What Are You to Me

A COLLECTION OF POEMS AND STORIES IN VERSE

VASANTHI VASUDEV

INDIA • SINGAPORE • MALAYSIA

ISBN

Hardcase 979-8-89415-976-8
Paperback 979-8-89277-957-9

Dedication

For all my family and friends, who read my poems from time to time and encourage me to write and share. This, my first book, is for you.

Scan the QR code and enter the password to listen to the poems and stories in the poet's voice

List of Contents

Gratitude *7*

Foreword *9*

01 Dominos 11

02 Ode to the Tavilkara 15

03 The Confluence 19

04 Integration 29

05 The Voice of Jasmines 35

06 The Cavern and The Moon 43

07 Born Again 51

08 The Silver Face 65

09 Into Those Eyes 73

10 Ballad of the Baluchari 87

11 The Freudian Slip 93

12 Topsy–Turvy 109

13 Jasmines Forever 115

14 What are You to Me? 125

15 From the Balcony 131

16 Yogic Connection....................143
17 With Velvet Gloves....................149
18 My Twin and I....................165
19 Towards Her....................173
20 Now at 43....................183
21 Those Pink Envelopes....................187
22 To Meet with Him....................203

Gratitude

I owe my deep interest in writing poetry to two persons, who were my muse, Dr. S. RamMohan –Indologist, writer and G. Balasubramaniam-former director, CBSE. Thank you!

A bow of gratitude to well-known writer and poet, Sreekumar Varma for reviewing my e-collection, 'Suspended Animation' and encouraging me to publish my poems in book format.

Many thanks to good friend, Giridhar Bail for organizing my maiden poetry reading session at Madras Gymkhana Club.

A big thank you to poet N. Suresh for the idea of doing a book with stories in verse and sharing some of his work with me.

Am very grateful to Saraswathi Srinivasan, Padmini Paramasivan, Rama Dhamodharan, Lakshmi Jayaraman, Lakshmi Rao, Rupa & Lalith for their valuable inputs that have enriched this book.

Thank you Bhavani Sitaraman for the book illustrations, Vasumathi Ramesh for the cover design, Sumitha Nath for editing and proof reading, Siddharth Das and C. Girinandh of Aura Studios for the audio recording, and Notion Press for the book publication.

Dr Vasanthi Vasudev

Foreword

From womb to grave, we wish to stay connected...be it to our physical environment of people, places and things; to our psychological space of thoughts, ideas and beliefs; to our metaphysical state of going inwards and connecting with ourselves, or with all of creation and with the creator!

This collection of poems and stories in verse, 'What Are You to Me' is about these connections; some of which grow into relationships. The opening poem, 'Dominos' sets the stage by describing the interconnectedness of life – how everything is connected with everything else. There on, poems and stories describe what may exist between many sets of twos: mother and child, a pair of twins, two sisters, two strangers, a young man and woman, an older twosome; a teacher and her student, the vendor and her customer, the dancer and the drummer, a maid and her mistress. Concluding in the same vein, the last piece in the collection traces the connection between a devotee and her Creator.

The dynamics of these connections / relationships sprout myriad moods: humour, excitement, anticipation, disappointment, love and peace.

I sincerely hope that these contexts and moods – poems and stories in 'What Are You to Me' – would draw you into an insightful experience of connectedness.

Dominos

Password: Listn22me?

01

Dominos

Preface

Everything in life and on this planet is inter-connected. Plant to animal, animal to man, man to woman – the cycle of the connectedness must go on…it cannot stand still. Using the imagery of nature, in the poem Dominoes, the poet describes the domino effect of a series of sudden happenings in the love less life of the protagonist who is stuck in a rut and has almost become a zombie. What happens and how do things change? Read on/ Listen in.

Poem

A stony mass sudden bolted
From somewhere
And splashed with the thud....
The moribund mossy waters,
A muddy morass,
Still and silent
For so many moons
Awoke with a startle...
The hibernating toad
-A proverbial 'frog in the well'-
Shifted its spongy webbed feet
And dragged a circle in the pond.

The silvery fish slumbering on its back
Jumped and looked up
It saw the moon beaming bright
On the summer sky, so very clear!
It smiled and frisked in the waters
Spiralling drunken zees....
And the pond burst with life
Once more.

He had sat, for ages now....
Shutting his gaze
To the world beyond the pond.
He wanted to see nothing, no one....
The movement in the pool
Stoked something in him;
His hands felt the softness of bamboo
As he pressed the reed to his lips.....
The waters rippled to tender music
Waltzing psychedelic fluorescence....
And the bounteous tree moved.
When lo!
A bark, laden with frangipani blossoms
Waxy and lush,
Fell on her wrist
As she stood by the pond, statuesque...
Frozen in dreamy tranquillity,
Half awake, half asleep....
She gently opened her hands

As her subconscious stirred...
She gathered the flowers....
And soaked into their fragrance.
Her feet, heady in scent,
Tapped and moved;
Now gentle, now fast
To his floating tunes;
The flowers flew from her hands
And sprayed the air....

He opened his eyes
To their satin touch
And in a blink, beheld her
In his wondering gaze.
Two hearts beat in symphony....
And the mighty forest swinging, swayed
Refreshed, it breathed in life
Ever more, again
Once again!

Ode to the Tavilkara

Password: Listn22me?

02

Ode to the Tavilkara*

Preface

Set in the rich imagery and idiom of Kerala, the poem, 'Ode to Tavilkara' traces the delicate nuances of a young woman's longing for closeness with her beloved, the tavilkara (the drummer). The romantic verse captures the yearning and describes vividly the many roles she is sworn to play, to be close to him. What is she finally willing to become? Poetic fancy knows no bounds. Read on/ Listen in.

Poem

Oh, that you were that *Tavilkara!
Beating temple drums to trebled chants in trembling frenzy…
And I, that ardent devotee
Who claps in awe at gods who perambulate
To the throb of your beat.

Oh, that you were that Tavilkara!
Rushing down slopes
The marriage procession dancing at your heels

And I that water girl with handfuls of coconut water
To gulp between your gasps.

Oh, that you were that Tavilkara!
Fingers parched and bruised at day long beat
And I, that flower girl
To bandage your palm with *'champaka' petals
Touched in sandal oil.

Oh, that you were that Tavilkara!
Returning home with *'Neipayasam'
– The offering to the gods-
And I, your home keeper
Who spreads rose watered leaves for a 'love-fed' meal.

Oh, that you were that Tavilkara!
Rehearsing *'Talas' at moonlight
And I, that nubile dancer,
Who tip-toes to your beat
My *'tulsi-packed' plait dancing into the night.

Oh, that you were that Tavilkara!
And I the *'tavil'
That hangs down your chest

Like a medallion proud
And waits for your touch!

*Tavilkara – drummer *champaka – scented flower; *Neipayasam – pudding made of rice and jaggery; *talas – rhythmic beats
*-Tulsi – basll plant *Tavil – drum – percussion instrument

The Confluence

Password: Listn22me?

03

The Confluence

Preface

'The Confluence' is a beautiful love story. In the life of the protagonist, the point of confluence between the Thunga and the Badra, bears great significance. Some life changing events happen there. What are they? Read on/ listen.

Story in Verse

For as long as
She could remember,
She had sat…
Sat on many a moonlit night,
On the stone platform
That bravely
Juts into the
Restless confluence……
The 'koodli sangama'
Where Tunga
Meets and merges
With Badra
And they become
The mighty one-
The Tungabadra.

And plunging headlong,
Onto her lap
At the confluence,
Had forever been
Mere child play!

It all happened
On that day,
The auspicious day,
Of 'Rathotsava'-
(Chariot festival)
When the village folk
The young and the old,
Who lived in
Mud and thatch homes,
Decorated them
With flower festoons
And five feet lamps;
Then donning their finest,
They flocked
Towards the temple street
That stretched up to
The confluence.

Gleaming silver and gold,
In the gaze of the full moon,
The majestic multi-colored chariot
Set out… lofty and proud!
And, every eligible bachelor

Waiting for his nuptial night
Showed off bare, sweaty sinews
Of shoulder and arm
As he heaved the temple car
And inched through the throng.

Every one of them did;
Everyone, but him…
He sat silent
He sat alone
He sat forlorn
On the stone platform
Rough and cold;
Facing the confluence…..
Having left the crowd
And his dreams,
Far behind.

That festive night
When the air
Was full of celebration,
Holding a brass plate
Laden with fresh blooms
She waded through
The sea of people…
And that was when
She saw him;
In a distance,

At the confluence,
His back facing her.

Scenes from the past
Swept swift…
Recollections of
Traumatic moments,
Of tender touch,
Came floating through…
How she had
Been caught…
Sucked fast
Into a whirlpool
At the confluence.……
How, in panic
She had gulped
Large sheets of water
And buckled into currents…

How she had swooned.
And when she had
Opened her eyes,
He was fanning her,
Holding her so close…
Lying in his arms
Feeling his hot breath
She had lost herself
In his deep, longing eyes
Soaking love.

Those moments
Froze…
They stood still…
His touch lingered,
Raising hair
On end.

That he was lost on her,
That he craved for her,
That she was
The one moon
That could light
His long dark nights,
Was an open secret.
A secret that every child
In the village, knew.
He had proposed
A few months ago…

But he was lame
Short in one leg!
Faulty in gait…
So,
How could she?

Yet… some remorse
And even a slight
Sense of guilt
Played hide and seek
With her pride
And fame……
She, after all,
Was the 'belle'
Of the whole village
And of ten and twenty
All around…
How could she
Accept his love?

Dismissing her thoughts,
She turned sideways
Away from him;
When, lo!
Her glance perchance,
Fell on an aged couple…
New faces,
Visitors, maybe…

The woman
Was short and comely
With a large sprig
Of fresh jasmines
Clumped on her
Greying hair;
While the man was dashing,
Tall and regal
In white *'dothie'
And spotless *'kurta'.

He was holding her
By the arm, gently...
His face, devoted,
Was fixed on her
As she slowly,
Wincing at every step
In unsteady gait,
Laboured her way
Towards the temple.

Statue like, in a stupor
She watched them
-The conspicuous couple-
So lost in each other,
Reach the temple...

He bent and helped her
Raise a leg

To cross the threshold
And the woman
Looked at him
Her eyes
Brimming adulation
In full.

At that moment
Unknowingly,
She too
Crossed the threshold…
She picked lightly
Her billowing skirt
And swirled around…
She made a U turn
Towards the platform
Where he continued to sit
Gazing at the confluence,
His feet dipped in the waters.

And before she knew,
Before she could stop,
Silver anklets
Tinkling all the way…
Her dainty feet
Propelled towards
And stopped
At the platform…

At that moment
At that confluence
He turned.
He saw her…
His face shone
A millions moons!
Just then,
The frisking Tungabhadra
Leaped in a shower
And drenched
Them, sudden,
With her blessed splash!

*dothie – wrap around – lower garment worn by men in India
*kurta – long upper garment like a collarless shirt worn by men & women in India

Integration

Password: Listn22me?

04

Integration

Preface

Carrying the psycho-spiritual construct of 'connectedness' in its core, the anecdotal poem, 'Integration', describes the dramatic shift in the protagonist's attitude that is caused by a random event. While waiting for a train, in an unfamiliar station, a series of actions and reactions result in some hard hitting realizations. What were they? Read on/ Listen in.

Poem

I sat alone
On the platform
Trains came
And they left…
I saw faces many
Knew not I, any.
I felt strange
Even a little fearful…
Why?
Was it the unfamiliar nature?
Of people, or place?
Who were they?
Were they different from me?

Yes and No.
Not really, yet, very.

They were humans like me
Yet, I did not feel a part of them
Social conditioning had taught me
The dictum…
'Familiarity is safe
Known faces are friends.'
"Stay away", it warned
"From the dangers of the unknown"!!
I was lost and rootless
Caught in the traps of my clichéd past.
I struggled to break free
To smile in friendship
To the faces by my side
But was it fear?
Maybe 'twas arrogance…
Or was it ego?
'I' felt separate
From 'we' and 'all'…..
I held back
Conscious of
Black and white!

Suddenly,
All hell broke loose
In twinkling time
I was in the thick 'RED'

Of mayhem
Amidst a crowd of 'Coolies'

Drunken calves
Swung in action
Shoulders knocked
Arms locked
Necks craned
Shrieking fear
Screaming pain.
And then,
My voice barked
Loud and bold
Soaked in empathy
For the victim
Spewing anger at the victor.

"Oh stop – Do stop!"
As my own 'unfamiliar voice'
Rent the air
And I stood
Shocked at everything
Including my outburst
And involvement...
Dead silence was born...
A dozen eyes challenged...
"Who are you?!!"
Angry stares
Fixed on

My two hands
Firm and strong
That tugged the victim
On to his feet.

The old man
Dragged himself to a stand
Leaning frail
On his bone
And my will!
My will to defend him!

At once
All friction ceased
Voices were lost, and
Heads bowed in shame.
At that split second
I became
A floating particle
Riding the wave of humanity…
Connected, intimate,
One!
Inseparable
From the cosmic sea
Of Collective Consciousness!

As I merged
And became one
With the milieu

The aged muscular figure
Held my arm tight
And steadied his feet
He lifted and tied
His fallen head cloth,
His red turban…
His black beady eyes
Shone and smiled…
Pupils singing
A prayer
Of gratitude….

Feeling integrated,
Full and whole,
I moved,
Brisk and bright;
Smiling in triumph;
I quickly picked
Hitherto scattered pieces
Of myself and my luggage
And boarded the train
To my destination.

The Voice of Jasmines

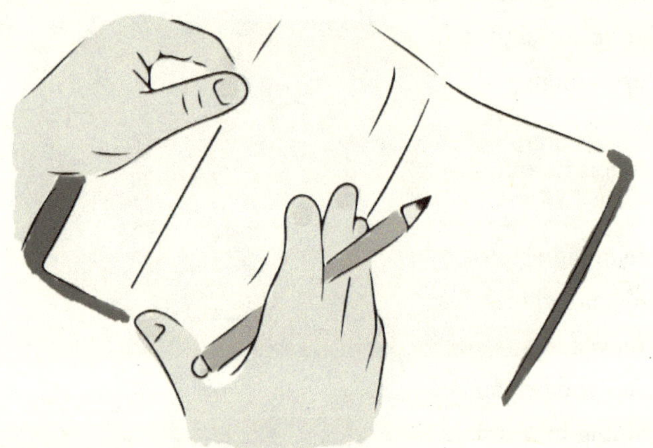

Password: Listn22me?

05

The Voice of Jasmines*

Preface

'The Voice of Jasmines' is a beautiful story about two travelers and their most unexpected bonding. The protagonist is a writer and he meets her, his fellow traveler, during a train journey. Who is she and why do her responses leave him awe stricken? Read on/Listen in to find out.

Story in Verse

The wheels of life
Trundled on,
Without a pause……
I continued to write
Pen on paper,
Without a pause…
Sheets of thoughts
Hope, smiles, angsts
Dipped in ink
Piled in stacks
Fluttered and shook
With the jumping wheels
Of the blustering train.

When Lo!
I was engulfed, tight
North – south, east – west
Everywhere…
In the grip of fragrance
Of jasmines white,
Fresh and crisp!

Suddenly, I came
Face to face
Breath-taking close
With beauty nonpareil…
Just here, so close,
Just in front of me
With jasmine buds
Adorning her black tress,
She silently sat……

In cavern like closets
Of my heart
Deep and secret,
I captured her beauty
And painted my verse
In captivating form and hue!

She did not seem to see me
Nor was I, anywhere in her presence…

She just sat and sat
She picked up
Sheets of white paper
Inked with emotions
And continued to read
Read me
In my verse
As her eyes darted
Left to right
And back again
Without a rest.

In speaking gestures
In acquiescing nods
In smiling lips
Set in silent motion,
She asked for more
More of my verse
More of my heart
Its song and tale....
Her eyes flashed
Like glow- worm
Her glance darted
Like quick silver
Her face, shone-
A full moon!

In that instant
She moved near…
She came
Came close, so close
And sat, beside me.
Intimate and cosy…
She sat with a sense of 'right'
As though
She had been there
Beside me
From that very day
Of creation…

She imprisoned me
In her jasmine veils
And I continued
To dissolve into
The fragrance…

Become one
With the jasmines
With her……
Even as she gently,
Gently stroked my pen
To style a title….
A title for my verse
On my page of life!
It read:
In Mute Chains

My insides wilted
As my heart cried
"Oh No!
My beauty is mute!"
But even unknown to me,
Just how-
I know not,
I heard my voice
Ring out
Clear and loud……

"Who is mute?"
I asked and answered:
"I speak in my verse
And you respond
In the flutter
Of the jasmine…
Your jasmine eyes!"

"And who is in chains?
You or Me?"
I asked…
Looking straight
Into my eyes
She just smiled…
Smiled from
Eye to eye…..

As I stood
Motionless and chained,
Chained in love,
In her voluminous silence,
I heard her
Sing and laugh
To the accompaniment
Of a million jasmines…
That bloomed everywhere
In my heart
Drowning me
In their soaking sweet voice.

This poem draws inspiration from a tamil poem by N Suresh.

The Cavern and The Moon

Password: Listn22me?

06

The Cavern and The Moon

Preface

In the humorous and allegorical poem set to rhyme, 'The Cavern and The Moon 'the poet describes the chase and flee that takes place between an aged man (cavern) and a free spirited young woman (moon). At a deeper level, the poem describes the futility of unreasonable desire – the moon being a metaphor for an object of desire and the cavern being someone who seeks and lusts for that object. What does it all lead to? Read on/ Listen in.

Poem

The cavern is old
Ancient, and badly bald.
For long, so moon struck,
Desperate is he, for change of luck.

In the evening he does wait
Be it early or so late;
Ranting loudly at the Sun
"Be gone, before I am all done"

His aching neck he almost breaks
For heart from head, never separates!

Upon the sky he does gape
Trying hard just to keep awake!

He laments ………

"Each day, she's so new,
Shimmering, in another hue!
Today, a big shiny face;
Then, she's gone without a trace!"

"When its pitch dark as hell
The sky's indigo as a well!
Where does she go and hide…
I've looked for her far and wide?"

As he moans and he sighs,
Lying in wait for 'her' so sky high,
In glides the fair and lovely moon
Nature's most magnificent boon !

Whenever she plays hide and seek
She makes him so forlorn and bleak …
Once more, he ponders so deep
And is quite again, about to weep.

"Wager, should I?
Bear refusal, will I?"
Emotions full and swelling fast
Fear to the winds does he cast.

In a full throttle, shaking like a blast
Snares himself into a net he has cast …
"O' Feisty friend, so dear, yet so far,
Don't tantalize me and deepen my scar!"

"It's time to come along,
My chest is deep and long.
My cravings are burning strong
And my home's where you belong!"

"Be comely in my cozy care
We do make a handsome pair!
To taunt you or to scare
None would ever again dare!"

"Why on such a lonely sky
Do you disappear from my eye?
Bright and brilliant like a bloom,
Gone into such ghastly gloom!"

"Grown thin in decline
It takes you long to shine ….
This cycle ever cycles
Stop must all these trifles!"

"Tireless tyranny needs to end
It's all just fine, don't pretend!

Such a suitor you will never find,
Ardent, anchored and ever so kind!"

The cavern so old became breathless, so,
His heart he outpoured nevertheless, lo!
All of earth and heaven, so remote
Did hear and echo his cringing quote!

But the silver maiden did not fumble,
Deafened ever, by his ever long rumble…
Never did she gasp, caught in a tumble
Instead, she whispered in hush and mumble:

'Oh! Can't he see how he looks,
So much like scary, vile crooks!
Bent back without shape,
A monster in a clownish cape!'

'Should I, to him, hold a mirror?
Show him how he's so queer?'
With mischief in her enchanting eye,
Dripping honey in her crooning cry:

"Ah! Your sweet words do now, belie
Far far away must I fleeing, fly!
If only I could be your worthy match!
Sadly though, my feelings aren't a patch!"

Not once at you have I ever shot
A fleeting glance, leave alone pinpoint!
Your primordial desire is so lusty hot!
Pray spare me! Push me not, into a spot!

But he would not stop ....

"O temptress white,
Refuse not! See my plight!
Words are sharper when thrown,
Than razor pointed stone!"

"Shatter not, to debris
My dressed dreams, in a spree.
Come and fill my waiting core.
Bond! And watch my yearnings pour!"

But she flared up in indignation........
"Aha! Be seduced and be damned!
No more can I withstand!
Scorched was I by Sun of lust
Merciless! Betrayed in every trust!"

"My face's so full of flaws,
Scarred by deceit's deadly claws!
Daughter of the cool oceans am I,
Dance with leaping waves do I!"

"Tip-toeing on ephemeral surf,
All the waters are indeed, my turf!
With such élan and verve,
The whole arc, I race and curve."

"Every bit, the free spirited blue,
Dodging stars without a clue!
Riding clouds pink and cream
Flying fancies on rainbow beam!"

"Chained in constancy to none
Fanciful; I do love to run…
Fickle, whimsical,
Quixotic, mercurial!"

"These and every tirade
I will own and trade.
To be a bound-less, bridle – less maid,
This, my final prayer, will never fade!"

The conversation never ceased….

Sulking, hurt and fiery red,
Still he tosses for her in bed…
His ego is holed and fully bled
Yet, he won't agree, he was misled!

Nonchalant, the moon, merry
Floats with joy extraordinary.

She tip-toes on clouds in a pile
And gushes a reckless rosy smile!

Is she mad? 'What's wrong with her?
Why does she refuse?'...he ponders.
'Oh, why does he moon for what he will never get?
Where do I go and hide, to make him so forget?!!'....she wonders!

The cavern on earth will forever look up and cry
But the moon won't ever climb down, from the sky
Their paths will never cross
No matter whose is the loss!

He the cavern, a cavern will forever, be
And she, the moon, only a moon will ever be!
The story of the cavern and the moon will never end
For, never does a chase and flee, bend or mend!

Born Again

Password: Listn22me?

07

Born Again

Preface

Born Again is a touching story of an innocent relationship between two people – a young boy and an old lady – who are different in every which way. What is the reason for the bond? Were they destined to meet? Read on/ Listen in.

Story in Verse

Wearing a checked saree,
A glowing, grassy green;
Bright glass bangles
Tinkling on dark hands,
A plump lady
With a big bindi, sat…
She sat
Cosy and smug
Right under the
Frangipani trees
That dotted
The jogging track
In the park.

Set, all around
Was her
Paraphernalia…
A bamboo basket
With unroasted channa;
Newspaper sheets
Cut and clipped
All around the edges
Fluttered 'pitter-patter'…

Fresh ripe tomatoes
Luscious, seductive;
Onions – peeled and chopped;
Bright green coriander
And sunny lemons
Laid out on plates
Arranged like *rangoli
Colorful and bright…

Sitting proud by her side,
Was a small kerosene stove
On which she placed
A black pan
And roasted
Crisp hot *channa
Or made channa chat*
A hundred times
For the slim – 'waisted'
Joggers who flocked

To the park.
I saw her at day break
On most mornings.....
When I, panting,
Dripping sweat
And cursing,
Counted aloud
The number of rounds
I had to jog
Before I could take
The tennis racquet
For a challenge!

She would call out
In a voice
Soft and persuasive
That sounded
Like a chirp,
Almost...

"Baba come over here...
Come and taste
My hot channa chat!'

I would hesitate...
She would canvas...
"Don't worry if you
Don't have a rupee...
I will keep a note

Of all your dues
And collect it one day
In full and full!"

On a good day
I would yield
To temptation
And make her
Effusive and ecstatic;
She would
Serve me channa chat
With special gestures
And try to give me a hug
If I came too close!

I would gobble up
The tangy channa chat
In a jiffy,
Bid adieu
And resume the jog
As though
The channa chat
Was my birth right.
Well! She made me feel
That it was!!!

On other days,
I would jog
Extra fast

And, as I approached her
Would run fast
Past her…
My face fixed on
The track
Her call,
"Baba, baba"
Was left
Trailing
In the air!

This game of
'Blow hot-blow cold'
Went on for
Six odd months…
It remained a secret
Between just the two
Of us!
Until, one day,
Amma got wind of it…

I had stuffed
My T-shirt pocket
With a handful
Of*'channa chat'
And forgotten
All about it!
The damn tell-tale!

Stiff interrogation followed:
'Where was the chat from?
Who was she?
Was it hygienic?
Maybe not…'
My tennis coach
Was spoken to
And thereon,
I ran
Only around
The tennis court
Under the eagle eye
Of the bullying coach.
That day on
I did not see her
Or indulge
In her tasty fare!

Sometimes I wanted to
Jog by the park
To see her,
To taste her chat,
But visions of
Amma's stern
Chiding face
Showed me
A red stick…
And it grew
Larger and larger

As I pushed the pedal
In her direction
And so, I would
Back off,
In quick reflex!

A few months passed
And it was nearing
Winter time…
That Sunday morning,
While I still lay
In bed
Amma woke me up
Looking rather flurried…
"There is an old lady
By the door
She wants to talk to you
She doesn't know you name
She is asking for 'baba'
Who is she?
Do you know her?"

Of course I did!
I jumped out of bed
And rushed to the front door.
She stood just outside,
In the passage
In the same
Grassy green saree,

Looking shy and sad.
I grinned broadly
And greeted her.
"Namaste *Ajji
How come
You are here
Did you come
To collect your money?"

Ajji moved her head
West to east
East to west
To say 'No'.
Instead, in a
Soft and sweet sounding voice,
She said:
"You did not
Come to eat my chat
For so long…
I missed you so much…
I had to ask so many
To get here."

She pulled out
A packet
She had been hiding
Under her saree
She held it proudly
Before me

Saying:
"I brought some
Fresh chat
For you"

My hands eagerly
Darted at the packet
When I heard Amma holler
"Stop right there!
I told you not to eat
That spurious stuff!
Do you owe her money?
Why is she here?"

Ajji's eyes welled
Ocean like,
A big tear rolled
On her dark,
Deep lined cheek…
Her breath became heavy;
She pulled back the packet
Looked at Amma
And said:
"Baba reminds me so much
Of my boy,
I lost him
In an accident
When he was just eight…

See this – look at him
He looks just like baba."

She pulled out
A black and white picture
A little torn
A little dog eared
And handed it
To Amma.
I lunged forwards
To see the picture…
A young lady
Was standing
Hand in hand
With a young boy
Yes! He did look
A bit like me!
Same height
Same nose, maybe…

By now, Ajji was sobbing
Saying: "Sorry, very sorry
I should not have disturbed
You or baba…
It's just that when ever
I saw baba,
I felt
My Raju was reborn
I wanted to give him

All my love
Feed him with all
I had!
I make very good chat
Very tasty, very clean"
She said
In crisp self-defense
Smarting in hurt and pain.

For a few minutes
Amma stood motionless
Then she gently
Walked up to Ajji
She took my hand
And placed it
On hers…
Her hands
Were still holding
The packet tight.
A small smile
Lit up Ajji's face
And Amma's too.

Slowly the air
Became breezy
And fresh light
Gave new life
All around.
I could see

The future
Unfold before
My eyes…
I now saw myself
Jogging fast
In the park,
Having a taste
Of channa chat.
How delightful
Had the day become!!
Wow!
What a second chance!
To be
Born again
Even whilst
I lived……

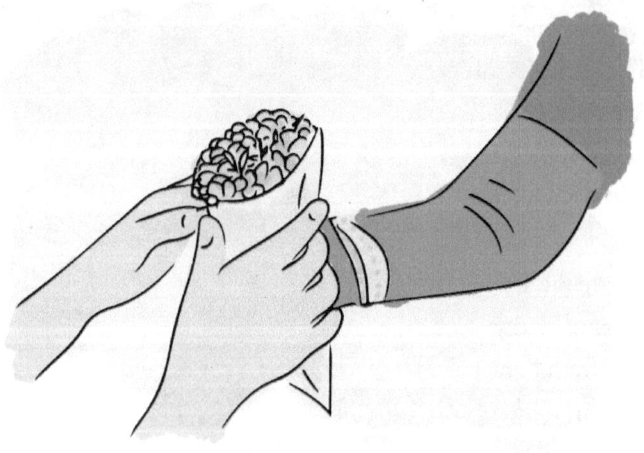

I opened
The packet
Of warm
Channa chat
With a
New found
Excitement
And triumph!

And, Oh!
Did I see
The same
Excitement and triumph
In Ajj'is gait too?
As she waltzed
Towards the elevator?

*Ajji – grandmother ; *Channa – broken chick peas; *Chat – a spicy Indian snack
* Rangoli – creative designs drawn on the floor

The Silver Face

Password: Listn22me?

08

The Silver Face

Preface

In the beautiful poem. 'The Silver Face', the protagonist describes her connection with a "silver face' that she begins to propitiate as part of custom and tradition.

Over time, her relationship with the silver face transforms into something very surprising. How does this happen? What is the power of faith and familiarity? Read on/ Listen in.

Poem

I was eighteen,
A blushing bride… when,
My gracious mother
Handed me a *silver face*
Wrapped in crisp white tissue
And placed in a beautiful cane box.
I opened and saw her, shining resplendent…
Jet black hair in waves were capped
In a golden crown studded with gems.

On long ear lobes,
She wore dazzling red earrings-
Her ear studs were a fiery red…
And on her long-chiseled nose,
Two lovely studs in red and white stones.
A lustrous pearl hung from the edge
Of the nose,
Touching, almost, her full upper lip,
That closed gently on the lower one, bud like.

She sported a black bead neck piece
That gripped tight, her doe-like neck.
On it were strung gold coins etched with tiny lotuses.
Her forehead bore a beautiful long streak
Of vermilion and turmeric.
Below slender, arched eyebrows.
Her eyes were round; piercing;
And she looked, straight, head on,
At me!

Mother, in a choking voice,
In one unending sentence,
In nonstop breath, instructed:
"Bring her out every year,
On the appointed day;
Place her on the silver pot
Filled with silver coins,
Rice and many things auspicious.
Wrap around a silken skirt

Shining, soft, and sequined.
And in your most precious finery
Bejewel her and lustrous make!

Sprinkle her, with scented rose water
And anoint her in fresh sandal paste;
Decorate her with roses and oleander....
Deck her in jasmines garlands
And precious gems.
Seat her in a rosewood canopy
With tender banana shoots
Tied on either side, like an arbour,
With lotus buds adorning the base.

Then light the silver lamp with five faces;
Fill the room with the fragrance
Of incense and camphor...
Now welcome her
To your home;
And into your heart
With a lilting song....
Pray and seek her love.
Ask for her blessings and grace
For a fortunate life."

I followed
My mother
In letter and spirit
For thirty long years...

I unpacked her,
Dressed and decorated her;
Sang to her;
Read out prayers
In salutations to her….
Sang to her
In her 108 names
Offered her sweets
And many delicacies
And put her back in the box
To sleep until the next year.
She was a welcome annual visitor
A familiar silver face!
And that is who she remained.

Then, that year,
I did not
Put her back in her box.
Instead, I let her
Be under the canopy
And made what I did
On the appointed day,
Once, every year,
Frequent habit.

I dressed her up,
Every Tuesday and Friday
In all regalia and finery
And kept her on center stage

In my home;
I saw her every time as I breezed
From one room to another…
I greeted her in the morning,
I bid good night, every night.
Before I went to bed.

Days and months,
Months and years passed…
Something unexpected began to happen…
Her taut silver face became soft,
Human like, she showed a change and more.
She was not the same, every day.
Sometimes, she smiled bewitchingly;
At times, she seemed somewhat grumpy.
Some evenings, she was a picture
Of grace and compassion;
And then, on another,
She was all calm and serene.

I began to notice how
Beautiful she looked
In her pink skirt
And then, when I put
A pearl chain on her neck,
She looked all dolled up;
So charming and spectacular!
She became my friend,
My alter ego; my confidante'…

My constant companion,
She accompanied me
When I travelled
Seated in that same
Beautiful cane box!

She was no longer
Just a silver face…
She was my eye
And my ear
My voiceless voice!
I spoke to her,
I cried to her.
I felt safe and comforted…
Her merciful, loving eyes
And her benign smile
Watching over me…
Flooding my consciousness
At all times…
Every minute,
Every day!

The silver face,
So full of life,
Breathed life…
Breathed courage
Into me
And enveloped me
In constant, cradling care.

The silver face transformed
And exchanged places
With my mortal creator,
Now, a 'memory in a frame',
Feted and feisty
Decorated and loved
The silver face,
My immortal, mother… became!

Into Those Eyes

Password: Listn22me?

09

Into Those Eyes

Preface

'Into those eyes', is a light hearted story-poem about infatuation. The protagonist is a middle aged woman who is smitten by a handsome stranger. How does her haunting infatuation change her life? Set in the backdrop of Goa, this interesting tale about human expectations and responses has a twist in the tail. Read on/ Listen in.

Story in Verse

I looked at him
For the first time
In the fish market
In the narrow lanes
By the sea
At Maposa.

The seasoned fisherwoman
Was artfully throwing
Slightly stale fishes
Into his basket....

His innocent eyes
Could not see into
Her stealthy ploy…
He waited patiently
For her to sort the worst
And toss them in!

I witnessed the drama
With interest
And felt a little sad
For him
But he seemed
Quite merry…
Donning a bright
Printed shirt
Green palm
Splashed on Orange …..
Florescent and bold!
He was tall and muscular
His 'coloured' hair
Brushed back
Fell lush and heavy
Onto his sturdy nape…

Standing just behind,
I could see his
'Inverted pyramidish' back
In full;

I heard
His voice, low pitched
Bass and baritone…
When he asked for the price
And handed in what was asked
Without a bargain!
I saw his face
Only when he turned…
Long eyes
Snub nose
Full lips…
I could not look into his eyes
As he fleeted a glance at me,
Mumbled a 'Good morning'
Bowed his head in half a courtesy
And left……

The scene at the fish market,
His shirt
His hair
His face
And all…
They rotated
In fast motion
And kept dizzying me…
Like a bee in a bower
Circling for more nectar, heady.

That night I had a dream!
He and I on the beach
Nudging close…
Stepping into each other's
Footprints
Sharing coconut water
With one straw
Me, stroking his
Flying hair
And tucking it
Under his cap…
He pulling me
Towards him
Whenever a big wave
Leapt at my feet
And me,
Falling fast
Onto his chest
And flinging
My arms
Around his neck!

The dream
Soaked into my days
And made me want
To shut out my reality…
To close my eyes

And to savour the scene
Again and again
And again!

He haunted me
To say the least...
I darted to the fish market
And hovered around
The same shop
Almost every day
Even when I had
No fish to buy!
Where was he?

Then,
One day
When I had almost
Given up,
I saw him
In the long narrow lane
Walking towards me
But there were
Dozens of men and women
People and things
Between us.
I wanted to fly past
And find my self

In his arms.
But how could I?

As he passed me
He half-looked at me…
I grabbed the moment…
And In a shaky voice,
I said:
"Hello, we met
At the fish shop
On that Friday
Two weeks back
I was standing
Just behind you…"

He gave half a smile
Was he laughing
At my nervousness
Or at my eagerness?
"Hmmmm… Yes I think I saw you
You, going to buy fish?'
I quickly moved
My fish laden basket
To the other side
And nodded my head
In excited yes.

At the fish shop
I took charge.
I ignored the
Fisherwomen's
Cheating hands
And chose the best
From a large basket
And filled his.
He looked happy.

The next time we met at the shop
He let me pick his fare…
Slowly over a couple
Of shopping meets
I gathered that
He had move to Mapusa
From Mumbai
He was around my age
And looking forward
To a retired life.
He did not speak
Of his family
And I did not
Dare to ask
Although I was
Dying to know.
Was he too

A single like me?
I was too afraid
To even guess…
Lest he was not!!

I got to know
That he lived
In one of those

Newly built cottages
A little away
From the beach
Amidst coconut palms,
Mango and cashew groves
But he never invited me
To his home.
While I looked at him,
Maybe 'gaping eyed'
Taking in every feature…
He never met me
In the eye…
He shifted his gaze
Away from me…
Away from my eyes;
When the fish
Filled his basket,
He was quick to
Bid goodbye
And leave…
As though
He had kept
A flight waiting……

I still would not
Give him up
He continued

To possess me
For some unknown reason.

By now, I was
Quite fed up
Of my thoughts
Quite disgusted
With myself
And my obsession!
Still, unable to console
My yearning heart,
In what had become
Set habit,
I was at the fish market
That Friday too
Like every other,
At the same hour.

My heart leapt
And my eyes shone
When I saw
'fluorescent green'
Drawing close
He was there!
He greeted me
With a beaming smile
And said:
"Will you help me

With the fish?"

He sounded excited
I could sense his happiness
In his voice and gait…
I mirrored his expectations
And zoomed to cloud nine!
I had won him over!
I was over the moon
And that was when,
He, excited, chirped:
"This is the last time
I will buy fish here,
I am going back
To Mumbai
I seem to like it out there…
Like Versova to Mapusa!"

My heart almost stopped
My hands dropped dead
Like the fish in the net……
I quickly plucked
All my castles
From the air
Hid them under my pride
And heard myself say:
"Oops! So sorry

I have to rush;
Someone important
Is expecting me"
I plastered a weak smile
And managed a fake wink....
I tried to dodge his eyes
But could not...

His eyes
Met mine
A powerful pull...
For the first time
I saw him
Looking into my eyes
Absorbing me in full
With interest......

Was it a little
Too late?
Or had I said
Too much,
Too early?
Had I moved away
Before time?

He stood
Lost in me
While I dragged
My steps
Away from him…
Leaving him,
Leaving the fish,
Lying in baskets
Silent and cold,
Waiting to be sold!

Ballad of the Baluchari

Password: Listn22me?

10

Ballad of the Baluchari*

Preface

*In enthralling rhyming verse, The Ballad of Baluchari narrates the passionate love of the lovely belle of *Baluchar for the young weaver who weaves his love for her in exquisite Baluchari. Sadly, though, her life takes a turn for the worse and the lovers are separated. What happens thereafter? How does their love find a resolution? Read on/Listen in*

Poem

i.

This is a tale of love: of living love that's not history
And it's woven all around a* Baluchari, along the Bhagirathi*.
On its bank she sat; swaying slender, silvery feet,
Anklets tinkling bubbles, with every beat.

The curved smile of the crescent moon
Brought nostalgic memories, bursting strewn…
His smile, his bewitching gleaming smile,
Came floating from many a distant mile!

Pink, blue, yellow, scarlet and green,
The Bhagirathi rippled; alit in every sheen,

Vying bold, paisley filled woven tapestry,
The lore filled 'pallu' of the feisty baluchari!
ii.
Her eyes moist as she closed them in daily dream,
The only dream; her night and day, dream…
He, amidst the mangroves on Bhagirathi's broad flank
His toe, tracing her name on moist sandy bank!

From his strong hands, fluttered and flew,
The softest weave telling stories, so many, anew.
He had woven his love in every warp and weft
Months of toil, oil lamps dripping steamy sweat.

Sweet passion for her shiny, twisted tress,
Her doe like, prancing pupils, fluttering an eager, 'Yes'!
Her pouting pink lips parted in high hot flush,
His baluchari, wrapped around her waist, so succulent, lush!

iii.
The seventh, girl child, an unwanted commodity;
She had been disposed of, regret-less, in a jiffy.
He, a weaver, the poor weaver's seventh son,
He had not had the price, to pay for his beloved one.

Her life had taken a deep, tumultuous tumble,
She had to forbear much, without a mumble.
The humdrum of a life so solemn and stoic,
Left her craving for love or a spark, heroic.

Her life turned worse when her 'man' so old,
Into jaws of death was drawn, crude and cold.
Twisted out of shape in destiny's severe jolt,
She returned; passions locked in double deadbolt.

iv.

But what did she comeback to, in barren midlife?
In whom can she lose herself and all wrenching strife?
The Bhagirathi, so full, yet, seemed so very empty
She sat on vacant banks alone, seeking him, aplenty!

She lost track of time, had no news of him;
The sun rose and set; lifeless days were long and grim.
Save her lingering dream, she had little else left;
Her eyes were swollen dry from nights bitterly wept.

Her dark black tress, now on her neck scraped
'S' like, swinging hips, now inverted 'L' shaped…
She sat; eyes dull and stony, crushed in dreary past
But her feet still danced for a dream long ago, cast!

v.

Racing past gentle breeze, she, sudden, heard,
Her name floating sweet and old passions, at once, stirred.
His voice, treble shrill, flitted over the gushing stream,
Bouncing bold, like the flashing, moon beam.

His balding, grey head and sober gait,
Still locked a young heart at any rate;

Not for a moment had he forgotten anything of her,
A hundred romantic rendezvous… not one, in a blur!

Oh! How he had missed her and pined on and on
For those moonlit nights, Bhagirathi banks upon!
Not even a goodbye; she had had to leave with another,
But lo! His fervent, flaming heart had felt nothing for any other!

vi.

Her heart missed a beat; it almost stopped…
When she saw him a foot away and her feet high hopped;
What did his sinewy hands clasp so tight?
Their dreamy future or the orange baluchari, bright?

The saree slipped from his hand, almost…
And fluttered in hers; hope resurrected, utmost!
In its sheer magic, they stood, spell bound and mute,
Then, in gush and sparkle, soared to lives, so transmute!

The beautiful baluchari danced, as nascent beginnings set sail…
Its splendorous motifs told many a moving tale.
The radiant moon, coy, behind silvery clouds did quickly hide,
As they drew close and the baluchari, on her, did, breath-taking, slide!

On its serene bank, they sat, rapt in an embrace so very sweet
She, his every music was; and he, her every beat!
This is a tale of living love; of a love that is not a history;
And it's woven all around this baluchari, along the beautiful Bhagirathi!!

*Baluchari – a variety of richly woven saree that originated in the village of Baluchar situation on the banks of the Bagirathi river.
*Bagirathi – river situated in Murshidabad district of West Bengal – India.

The Freudian Slip

Password: Listn22me?

11

The Freudian Slip

Preface

Does time stand still? What happens when two lovers who have drifted apart, meet again? The story in verse – 'Freudian slip' describes the bonds the protagonist feels and the dilemma she goes through in understanding herself and her connect with a man she had fallen in love with years ago. How does she succeed in finding her true emotions and herself? Read on/ Listen in.

Story in verse

That Monday morning
Started with a startle…
On my desk,
At work,
Was an invite
For cocktails & dinner.
To meet
Ajit Patwardhan
The new Vice President
Of 'Hamsa media mix'!
I picked up the invite
Slowly, and reeling
As in a trance,

I sat
With a thud
On my swivel chair.

My world spun
And swirled, so sudden!
Memories, floating,
Rushed in…
On Fridays evenings,
Nudging close,
Feet flying in the air,
We would perch
Above the rocks,
On narrow stone walls
That guarded the waves
Along the *Marine Drive…

Grabbing chat at *Chowpatty
After a good run
On Sunday mornings;
Travelling in crowded trains
Holding each other…
Calling it a night
After a second show
At Regal cinema
And munching
Roasted corn-cobs
On the way back!

Flashes of images,
Slices of conversation,
Myriad moods
Rosy reminiscences
Of a heady courtship
That ended abruptly
Five years back,
Began to haunt
Once again……

The next few days
Were like
The last few days
Before going into labour…
When you can't wait
For it all to be over with!

And then, I met him
Over cocktails and dinner.
He was
Totally taken aback…
As though a
Cloud had burst
On his head
Full and full
Out of the blue!
We both
Did not speak
To each other

Except for exchanges
Of courtesy.
And then,
Two days later,
The inevitable happened…
He called
And wanted
To meet me
In an old
Rendezvous point…
A coffee shop
We both loved.

The Hamletian dilemma!
To be (there) or not to be
What should I do?
He had suddenly left me
Without word or explanation…
'To study, somewhere abroad.."
I heard
A 'bird' say!

Devastated, feeling jilted,
I had dragged myself
To move on
Eventually……
Yet, cinders of
Smoldering anger
Continued to burn……

I had cut all bonds
With him…
But it still ached…..
More than all the pain
Was the pull….
His magnetic charm
His wit and humour,
They still stole my heart
And made me weak…

But, I decided to be brave,
To meet him in the eye
To face the real-
The present…
We chatted
Over streaming cups….
Stories of childhood.
Of work,
About interests,
About everything
Except one…
Carefully dodging
The question
That towered
In the mind
Neither did he
Nor did I
Bring it up…
Although I

Was bursting to ask…
"Is there a special one"?

He invited me
To join him
On the ferry
To Elephanta caves
On Sunday
But I did not promise
To go.

The next few days
Were a torment…
Something made me
Want to go
Although I knew
That it could be
Fraught with danger
I could succumb
To his charm
All over again…
I walked on the precipice
Floating between illusion
And reality
The past alluring but distant
The present, as it was – real,
And the future?
What did I want?
Dare I investigate?

I moralized to myself
But yielded to temptation…
I threw
All logic to the winds,
Cast aside caution
And put
Out my foot…

Tingling in excitement
Crazy in attraction…
'It's just for a
Few hours;
Great place
For a day out…
The Elephanta caves'…
I convinced myself.

I met him
At Gateway of India
Amidst a hundred pigeons
Pecking at each other
Without a pause…
We found a ferry
And sat side by side…
I tried not to sit close.
I placed my tote bag
In between…
He looked at it
Tried to lift it off

I pressed it down
In protest
And he let it be……
Had anything changed?
Nostalgia lingered
Strong and perfumed……

I looked at
His silhouette
And my heart
Leapt a beam!
He was still
So appealing
My pulse quickened…
My heart throbbed!
I wanted to
Sing along
As he hummed
An old favourite number
He hadn't forgotten…
He tapped his fingers
On my bag
Just as he would
On my lap,
Years ago…
He seemed
The same…
Frozen in time.

I had to steel myself,
Fight myself
And sit still.

At the caves
It was déjà vu…
We strolled around
Beaten paths
Trespassed
Boundless memories
Criss-crossed into
Each other's space
In every step
In every bend…
We read
All the history
Admired every sculpture…

Right through
I did not say much
He was his zestful self
Talking about
His interesting
Days in Boston
His thesis
His network
And I,
An ardent listener…

We did not
Cross the Rubicon
Never asked
That 'big' question.

Over time,
He became quiet;
Pensive and watchful…
A little wistfully,
He observed me
Time and again…
I wanted to tell
Him all about
My life
'I will wait until
I know fully
How I feel
About him'
I thought
And restrained
My impulse and urge
To burst open…

The red-orange sun
Was playing hide and seek
With the waves…
It was* 'aarthi' time
And a huge crowd

Had assembled
Before the three-faced Shiva.
We stood
At the head
Of the crowd
Just in front of

The colossal Shiva's
Magnificent face.
I closed my eyes
And joined the echoing chant
'Om Shivaya Om'
The bells tolled in rhythm,
The sound of cymbals
Lashed against
The walls of the cave
And clanged a din.
I could feel his breath
Mingle with mine
I kept my eyes
Tightly shut
And struggled
To focus…
And then,
A few minutes later
I felt
Cool breeze
From the sea
Hit my nostrils…
I did not open
My eyes
To see if
He was still there.
I continued to chant
'Om… Shivaya

Namah Om'......
I lost track
Of time.
Feeling rejuvenated,
When I opened my eyes,
The sun had descended
Into its earthy bowel
The purple sky
Was tinting black...
The bell and cymbals
Had grown quiet
The whole cave
Was hazy in the
The bluish smoke
Of burning incense sticks...

I turned and looked
Left and right
Side to side
For him,
But he was not there.
I looked behind
And beyond
In the crowd
Of tourists
Crawling all over
The cave
Like giant ants...

The shadows
Were growing longer
The cave was growing dark too.
I still could not see him
I felt a little anxious
And before I knew it
I heard my voice, shrill,
Ask and echo:
"Suneel, where are you?
Can you hear me?
Suneel...?"

The questions reverberated
In the air,
Hitting the pillars,
Colliding with
The mighty Lord......
I bit my lip in shock,
In that moment of reckoning,
Of truth..
Of epiphany......
As I heard my
My subconscious speak......!
The Freudian slip
Was still ringing
In my ears

When he appeared
From the shadows
Of the tall pillars…

His face was fallen,
Dark like the bats
Echo locating and screeching
All over the cave……
As he staggered towards me
I heard his voice
Now cold and clipped:
"Your Suneel is not here; Only I am."

*Marine Drive & Chowpatty -Marine drive is a popular promanade along the sea front in Mumbai and Chowpatty is a public beach adjoining the marine drive in Mumbai, India

Topsy–Turvy

Password: Listn22me?

12

Topsy–Turvy

Preface

Set in the backdrop of the Covid pandemic, this humorous poem vividly captures the many entitlements that we seem to consider as a given and questions some dependencies that we have taken for granted. What happens when the old order changes and age old equations are challenged? What startling realizations happen when everything goes topsy – turvy ? Read on/Listen in.

Poem

The grey sink brimmed and choked
With pots and pans, it was yoked.
Everything was piled and heaped atop
Not even a drop could trickle nonstop!

Untidy stacks of cups and plates,
Dishes, black and burnt straight
Left overs floating like garbage, grimy
Swimming in the mess, silver spoons tiny !

Bits of paper, torn and thrown on the floor,
Water and syrupy potions, spilt near the door!
The bed was a heap of pillows and quilt
Sheets piled on top, just about to tilt!

Yesterday's shopping in brown paper jackets
Jostling for space with dozens of packets.
The dining table had the whole household:
Pens, needles, books 'n bottles – more than it can hold.

Four buckets of clothes – some soiled, some without a pair
A sock here, a scarf there, towels just about everywhere.
Shirts inside out, sleeves coiled and rolled
Clothes on the floor, more than in cupboards all told!

"Did the doorbell ring? It must be her, I bet
Oh! No! It's a quarter to seven; no sign of her as yet!
Weekend's over, the house is in such a mess
With every passing minute, up zoomed my distress!

Mumbling, I waited, bated breath, heart on the bell.
She did not come. Covid, instead, did-… like a bomb shell!
Life somersaulted and fear mounted ten fold
I could not let her cross over my threshold!

The sink, the floor, buckets and all
Accumulated piles like towers, about to fall

I put on my apron. I had to get started.
"It will take a while, but 'twill get sorted".

"What's in cooking and cleaning the muck?
I can do it, don't have to pass the buck!"
But lo! My clumsy movements and two left hands!
Startled, I exclaimed "Gosh! Does she wave a wand?'

My body bent; clothes fully drenched;
I worked until my heart wrenched.
For hours on end, I laid in bed,
Nursing my wounded nerves and head.

From then on, I counted every spoon
Before I cast it in the sink, too soon!
"Why do you need a large plate?
Let's have 'bowl – food', its rather late!"

"Careful! Don't take a new one, then…
This shirt's just fine, why don't you wear it again?
Walk slowly, the soup, don't spill
To clean and tidy up, it will surely kill!"

I sounded strange time and again
Was I becoming senile, or rather,sane?
Whatever… I didn't bother to explain
I just wanted her back, sun or rain!

Covid left me without her, high and dry
Straddling a million chores, life drudged by
I waited for the pandemic to wane
For her to come back to work again!

If only she would bring my morning tea,
And leave my home, sparkling to a tee!
What if she comes in a trifle late?
She's worth in gold, her every pound of weight!

When will the doorbell ring?
Will she come to work or at least ping?
I can't do without her; this is so true
I hate to concede it... But must give her, her due!

Jasmines Forever

Password: Listn22me?

13

Jasmines Forever

Preface

A picture in the newspaper sets the protagonist off on an emotional journey. What is it and why? Read / listen to this beautiful, nostalgia filled, love story to tune into his story about her and the jasmines.

Story in Verse

I saw her picture
In the newspaper…
Bordered in black;
Her face, at eighty eight
Had grown lines,
Some deep and furrowed
Yet, its beauty
Like precious pearl,
Had a lustrous glow.

She had
Left me,
Decades ago
Still… her shadows
Shadowed me.

They continued to,
For sixty years…
And nostalgia
Nascent, sweet.
Hung on
Like the lingering
Feel of honey!

My mind
Jogged back
To those halcyon days
When she was
Elegant, at eighteen
And I,
Handsome and eligible,
At twenty two.

Nymph like,
Draped gracefully-
A striking saree
Hugging her
Lissome form;
Her long
Plaited locks
Frolicking in fun
Behind slender waist…
Silver anklets, dainty,
Tinkling on velvety feet,
She would enter
The festooned

Eastern gate
Of the temple
At the stroke
Of five......
On the dot
For evening *'aarthi'

Wiping dust
Off my dress
And sweat off
My brow,
I would
Hastily drop
My bicycle
Near the
Peepal tree
And rush in
To be on time...
To be near the sanctum
When she entered!
Looking grand and regal.

On that blessed day,
I had bought jasmines
For the Goddess
And had placed them
On the ledge
Of the stone pillar
Outside the sanctum,
To free my hands,

And adjust my dhoti.

Forgetting to take them
From the ledge,
I had moved ahead
Towards the sanctum.
When I remembered
And turned towards
The pillar,
I saw her
Folding the jasmine string
And neatly tucking it
Into her plait…
Had she seen me
Place the jasmines
On the ledge?
Was it a symbol?
Of acceptance?
Her acceptance of me?
Oh!
How the jasmine flowers
Gleamed…
Set high
On her braid
So beautiful...
White on black!
Thus began a ritual
That lasted a whole year!
I never missed
Placing the jasmines

On the ledge
And she never missed
Decorating her plait
With their perfumed splendour.
The highlight
Of my evening
Why, my whole life,
Was that ritual
So sacred, so full of hope.
It coloured my dreams
And I flew happy kites
In realms so high!

We never exchanged
A single word
We only did,
Jasmines and smiles.

Until that fateful day
When the ritual abruptly,
Almost rudely,
Halted and ceased.
The jasmines
Lay tearful
On the ledge…
Left alone,
Like an outcast.

For the first time,
I mustered courage

To speak:
"The jasmines
Are cold, on the stone!
They are dying
Without your warmth"

She lifted her head
To look at me
And blurted hurriedly…
"I cannot
Accept them
For I cannot
Have them
Anymore…
I am spoken for…
Spoken for
Another man."
I heard a faint voice,
Incoherent and pained.

Her face was red
Like fire
Her breath,
Fast and hurried,
Knocked on
Her heaving chest.

Even before I could
Blink an eye
She was gone…

She had slipped
Into the crowd
And disappeared!
I never saw her again....
At the temple
Or anywhere.

The jasmines
Were left
On the silent pillar
To wilt and grow brown...
And on the
Following evening
The stone pillar
Looked empty...

Inauspicious
And abandoned,
As was my heart.

This morning,
I had picked up
Some strings
Of jasmine
Left by the flower girl
On the threshold
Along with
The newspaper,
As I usually did,
Every day.

But when I opened
The crisp sheets
Of newsprint,
Lo! Behold!
I saw her
Looking into my eyes.
My hands trembled
As they touched her…
I placed her
Softly, gently,
On my writing table;
Time stood still…
I was lost for a while
In her.
Then, slowly…

With heavy heart
And rushing breath,
I garlanded her
With the string of jasmines…

As they kissed
And adorned her…
The jasmines
Flashed a smile
And filled the place
With their scent…

Her intoxicating memory
Engulfed my being…
A hot tear
Huge and wet
Rolled down
To a drop
And hugged
The jasmine flower
With the hope
Of keeping it fresh
Forever!

What are You to Me?

Password: Listn22me?

14

What are You to Me?

Preface

The poem, 'What are you to me? 'is an exploration of how to define a relationship that exists between any two entities. Does definition bring greater clarity to the relationship? Must it be defined to commit to it? Is commitment conditional? The poet takes the broad canvas of life to expand on these questions and to arrive at some touching conclusions? What may they be? Read on/ Listen in.

Poem

The tender tendril asked the mighty oak,
'Are you my strength?'
The dazzling sunflower asked the burning sun,
'Are you my guide?'
The rising wave asked the milky moon,
'Are you my inspiration?'
The gleaming raindrop asked the dusty earth,
'Are you my destination?'

The floating feather asked the flowing wind,
'Are you my cradle?'

The hanging fruit asked the bending bough,
'Are you my protector?'

The flaming flower asked the springing fragrance,
'Are you my identity?'

The uncaged bird asked the limitless sky,
'Are you my freedom?'

The sonorous song asked the lilting tune,
'Are you my melody?'

The golden harp asked the taut string,
'Are you my symphony?'

The dreamy eye asked the clinging memory,
'Are you my consciousness?'

The lighting lip asked the sparkling smile,
'Are you my beauty?'

The tinkling anklet asked the silky foot,
'Are you my anchor?'

The youthful mother asked the newborn life,
'Are you my pride?'

The excited child asked the ephemeral bubble,
'Are you my joy?'

The drunken painter asked the visage on the canvas,
'Are you my soul?'

The nervous gambler asked the unknown future,
'Are you my prayer?'

The devout pilgrim asked the anointed idol,
'Are you my creator?'

The questing philosopher asked the fleeting moment,
'Are you eternity?'

The doubting self, asked itself,
'Are you an illusion?'

And, the candle asked the flame,
'Are you my hope?'

And night asked day,
'Are you my life?'

And then, She asked Him,
'Are you my beloved?'

Hearing no reply, they all hummed
In choral refrain…

"WHATEVER YOU MAY BE TO ME,"….
"WHAT EVER YOU MAY BE TO ME
LET ME GIVE UNTO YOU
MY ALL!"

From the Balcony

Password: Listn22me?

15

From the Balcony

Preface

In this interesting story – poem, a random view from the balcony marks the beginning of an emotional roller coaster ride. Where is the protagonist's ride headed? What does she wish for? Will that happen Read on/Listen in.

Story in Verse

One evening,
I saw him
From my balcony
As he walked
With an airy gait…
He stopped
Just below my balcony…
And pulled out his mobile
To take a call.

There was something
Striking about him
I braced myself

Against the railing…
And moved forward
To get a better view
Of him.

He was tall and muscular
Broad shouldered and brown
In his middle age
I could see his goatee
As he moved his face
While talking…
His voice sounded deep
I could not see
His face or his features
In full.
But something stirred
Deep within.

The next evening
I saw him again
Around the same time
But he did not stop below
My balcony.

A whole week went by…
I saw him every evening
At the same time.
But I still did not see

His face.
He never looked up
To see me
Standing in the balcony
Leaning on the railing……

That Monday,
Before I stepped on to the balcony
I combed my greying hair
Stuck a big 'bindi'
On my forehead
Wore a shiny, white blouse
And draped my favourite
Pale pink linen saree
That had red roses
Embroidered all over.

When I saw him approaching
My balcony,
I turned up
The sound of music...
I leaned against the edge
Swinging my arms into the air.
I heaved myself high
And hung my waist
Beyond the railing
Into the open!
Suddenly, a voice boomed
"Oh my God! What are you doing?
Do you want to drop down and.........?
Oh my God!"

I had succeeded
In winning his attention!
And that was when

I saw his face in full
His long aquiline nose
His broad fleshy lips
Crowned with a thick moustache
His deep black eyes
Well shaped brows
And expansive forehead…

Face, flushed
And sweaty,
And my heart
Missing its rhythmic beat,
Not one, but, many.
I pretended to be shocked at my self
And apologised for my recklessness.

That was the start
Of a conversation
With him
Which went on…
And on…
In my head
In my dreams…
At all times
Consuming me.
I spoke to him
About myself
My hopes and my fears

My highs and lows
My pains and gains
My loneliness,
My needs
My desires
My dreams…
But who was he?
What was he to me?
That I did not know
But I waited
Every evening
Holding the railing
Of my balcony
For him to come.

He would come
Every evening
I would wave to him
Gustily
In the hope
That he would
Begin a conversation
But he would not
Look up
On most days…
On some days
He gave me half a smile

Or half a wave
And kept walking
Away from my balcony.
Yet, I waited,
Waited for him
On my balcony
Every evening…

Two weeks later
I saw him
With an attractive woman
Were they holding hands?
Maybe… they were….
They looked
Touching close
Of each other!
I pulled away
From the railing
As though
I had been stung
By a scorpion.
I dropped down
Clumsily….
On to the floor.
I hid so that
They could not see me.
Why?
I did not want her

-The intruder-
To see me
No of course not
What happened,
From the balcony
Was something
Between us;
Only, He and Me!

With a twinge
In the heart
I watched them
Whisper and walk
Away from me.
I saw them both
The next day
And the next.
I stopped going
To the balcony.
At that time

I struggled to stay
Away from him
To not get a glimpse
Of him....
I denied myself
That joy
The feel

Of excitement
The adrenalin rush
The throb of my pulse
That titillating feeling......
Instead,
I sat in my room
Before the TV
And sulked...
When the sun
Went down
And it was almost dark
Only then, did I step
On to my balcony
But my spirits
Remained down
In the dumps.

And then,
On that day,
Some weeks later,
There was a knock
At my door
In the evening,
At that same time...
The same time
I used to see him
From the balcony....

My thoughts
Zoomed in auto mode....
He appeared
Before me....
I imagined him
Standing at my
Front door...

I opened the door
And presto!
It was true!
He was there
All by himself
He moved forward
Blurting;
"Oh! Thank God
You are fine"

In a trance,
I stepped back
And moved sideways
Into the balcony
I stretched my left arm
Up to the railing;
I gipped it firmly
And faced
The front door.

He was there
At the threshold,
Our eyes met
And in that instant,
I heard myself say:
"Do come in"

Yogic Connection

Password: Listn22me?

16

Yogic Connection

Preface

The humorous, anecdotal poem 'Yogic connection', set in rhyming verse, describes the admiration of the protagonist for her yoga teacher who changes her perception about Yoga and converts her to its practice, The connection now extends way beyond yoga. How does this transformation happen? Read on/Listen in.

Poem

Yoga they said:
"Is best at break of day. Well before the heat.
It's not for them, who at dawn, hide under a sheet!"
"Indeed", said I: "Not for me!"
"It's not for those who, into nights do toil
Burning waxy midnight oil;
Tiny drops that trickle forlorn,
Into cacophonous dawn!"

"Besides...
What good comes of Yoga, lo?
Why at all, do we need it so?
When yoga dulls and throws
Fun and frolic to a close?

"To strain and to stretch
A finger or a limb! O' wretch!
And 'statue like' do we freeze
Moaning for aches to cease!"
While the clock merrily ticks
And time drags on without a kick!"

I carried on…
"O! Why breathe in and touch the nose?
Then, breathe out and touch the toe?
To straighten a shoulder
Stand still like boulder?
No! Never!!
There's nothing as peppy
Better still, as chirpy…..
As a 'work out' in the gym
Where there's a machine for every whim.
What can be better?
To make me a lot fitter?
As beating in step
With dumbbells, instead?"

My claim did one day fly
When saw HER in action, did I!
Giving commands without a falter
Her sculpted pose, never to alter!
Tall and poised, she was well assured,
Twists and bends, perfect tens …and was I floored!

'Curiosity kills the cat' it seems…
Rope in hand, on the mat, was I seen!
For no one else on earth
Would I, even for a million worth!
Rise and fall
Upon a call.
Bend and buckle
Without fickle;
Stand on one leg
No support, no peg!
Hold my breath for long,
Lie like a corpse so strong!

And all in just a jiffy,
Her commands, never iffy!
With eagle sharp eyes
Her gaze all over flies.
On my every move,
Every pose to prove.
I daren't shuffle
Not a hair, ruffle.
Twitch a muscle, nor
She's ordered a pause, for!

So sensitive is she…
Seldom does she miss a wee.
A raise in my eyebrow,

Or a wrinkle on the brow!
She senses it, before it can grow;
The pain to go; and for me to glow
Quick remedies do pronto flow.
In some *'aasana', sure and slow!

Her persistence paid off in time,
Yoga is now, my interest prime.
With every bend.
Every stretch and mend.
A relief known just to some,
Yoga has such comfort, become!
The session goes far and deep.
Every pose and every leap;
Is so vital for my sleep!
Yoga's forever, precious keep!
My body, so very light,
Ever ready for a flight!

But, all this, besides and beyond,
Of her I've grown so very fond
Our ties are so taut,
Our bond, a tight knot.

The connection so much more,
Than any *'yogasana' core!

*aasana – pose /position of the body
*Yogasana – a yoga pose

With Velvet Gloves

Password: Listn22me?

17

With Velvet Gloves

Preface

With Velvet Gloves is a story poem full of pathos. It traces the turbulent relationship between two sisters who are very dissimilar. They meet after many years in an unexpected setting and circumstance. The story poem describes the thoughts and feelings of the protagonist, the younger sister. What happens when she sees her older sister? Read on/ Listen in.

Story in Verse

Through large windows
Dressed in pink curtains,
I could see
Those glorious stippled mountains
With touches of wintry snow…
As they stretched
Their long neck
Up to the edge
Of my room……

Resting my back
On a pile of pillows
I lay, uneasy,
On the high
Hospital bed
And tossed restlessly
On crisp sheets…

By my bed side,
In a wooden crib
That rocked,
Up – down
Slow and gentle,
Wrapped bundle like,
A tiny figure
Was sleeping sound…
My daughter
Full of nine
Days old!

Looking down
From my bed
Into the crib,
I could see
Her tiny eyes
Shut tight
As she slept…
Without a care…

In a smocked
Pink frock
With hoodie
And booties to match,
Snuggled up cosy
In a rosy world
Of baby bolsters
And 'hug-me' pillows,
She looked picture-perfect…
And I was lost in her.

I don't know for how long,
When an elegant visage
Crossed my eyes;
I lifted my head
And that was when
I saw her!
I saw her
So tall and stately
Full of middle age grace
Sporting a tan bomber jacket;
Her copper coloured hair
Covering her shoulders…
She did not
Look at me..
Her full focus
Was on the
Bundle of joy
In the crib.

I looked at her
With shock
Shock of seeing
Her so suddenly…
Her silhouette
Drifted fast,
Across decades
And tossed
A million
Images in my cloudy head……

She was my elder
By nine years,
To the date…
Who ruled
And herded,
Mentored
And coached
With indefatigable energy…
She handled me
With strict caution
And unwavering vigil…
With an iron fist
In a velvet glove.

More so
When I entered
My stormy teens

And that was how
It remained……

My mind raced
Back in time
And like
An electronic chip
Loaded with data,
It scanned
Two-decades
Of experiences…

Nineteen odd years
Had been too many...
Too many indeed,
To share and bond
With her;
A sister
So different
From me…
We, like chalk and cheese
Were quite unconnected
In age, outlook
Interests and habits…
And so, naturally,
Poor companions
By every stretch and measure!

"Climb down that tree! Now!!
Stop being a tomboy!"

"Who are you going out with?"
"If you are not back by ten,
You will get grounded
For a whole month."
"You are too young for this;"
"Are you done with you lessons?"
"Are you going to tattoo?
Yourself all over?"

Her voice bellowed
Loud and clear
So fresh,
As though it were
Yesterday!

Naughty skirmishes
Ugly bouts of temper
Dialogues and disagreements
Ending in sullen grief
Followed by long spells
Of communication black out!
Lock down time
And each,
Blocked in our own spaces!

Sharing a room
With her was
So suffocating
That at regular intervals,
On and off,
I preferred
To rejoice
In the airless attic-
Stuffy but free!

I was hell bent
On finding a way
To escape
Her polished
Chafe and chide
And then, one day,
I escaped.

I ran away from her
And everyone else…
I ran away
One night
To feel the fresh air
Of Santa Fe,
To paint
The desert;
The dotted bulges
Of rock and green stubble,

The Juniper trees,
The Pine, Spruce and Fir…
I ran away to taste life
Unbridled, unfettered!

New found freedom
Was fun, indeed!
I made new friends
And the night
Was always
Young and merry!

At times, the ride was bumpy
And I did lose sense and direction!
My daughter was
Nature's gift
To be borne and delivered
Alone…

I was convinced
That she,
By now, hated me
She may, with reluctance.
Own me
But that too
Only with embarrassment!
I did not hate her
Rather, I must admit

That I
Admired her focus
Her strength,
Her determination
To be prim and proper
To be right to the 'T'

But I liked myself too…
Careless and carefree
Emotional, gullible…
Friendly to a fault!
Indeed! T'was
Not our choice
That nature had
Made us so apart!

With a head full
Of memories
Of her and me
And our shared past,
I scanned her
Up and down
Thoroughly…
She had not changed
In the ten years
That had passed
Middle aged
Belly tyre,
May be hiding

Under her bomber jacket
Bur she was still
That angel faced beauty
Alright...
Was she still
Soft from the outside
But hard and firm
In the inside
Mindful and resolute
A role model
If any?
I wondered...

She walked up to me
Said nothing...
Not even a smile
In recognition,
Leave alone
Bonding...
She placed
An envelope
On my chest
And turned towards
My baby in the crib.

She fondled her
Very gently,
Whispered into
Her ear

Played with her
Tiny hands
And gently
Guided her
Index finger
Into my baby's
Soft fist.
I saw my baby
Close her fist tight
And my sister
Stood statue like
Unable to move
Tied in bonds of love
Wrapped around
Her finger!

I opened the envelope
And in it, I found ten cards…
Cards handmade and signed
Drawn and coloured
With crayons, bright!
My cards for her birthday
Year after year
When things
Between us
Were still
In place……

My eyes swelled
With tears
Those well
Preserved cards!
Every one of them!
Did she love me?
Somewhere
In the corner
Of her heart?
Why had she
Preserved them
For so long?
Did she know
That I had cancer?
I was wasting away
The bells were about to toll?

My eyes flashed
At her, near the crib
Still being held
By the little finger
In her palm…
She continued
To look
At my daughter…
Eyes fixed
On her
With a smile
On her lips.

I heaved a sigh-
Was it of relief?
I smiled at the paradox……
My regal sister
Being held captive
By my little daughter!!
Life sure,
Had a way of
Coming a full circle!

Strangely, I felt
Calm and assured…
My restlessness
Abated…
Upon seeing
My sister,
I knew
My little one
Would not be forsaken…
She would be safe
With my sister;
If I were
Gone……
And that thought
Was enough…
Nothing else
Semed to matter
In the least…..

Somewhere deep down,
Something stirred
Like a flutter…
What was it?
Was it a secret wish?
For putting the clock back?
Or was it
A yearning
For the safety
Of her velvet gloves?
Now, when it was
A tad too late?

I let out a sigh
And let all conflicts go.

.

I looked again,
Once more
At the two of them
To savour the scene
Of her with my her..
I closed my eyes
And breathed into the moment
With immense joy
And new found peace.

My Twin and I

Password: Listn22me?

18

My Twin and I

Preface

How does it feel to be born with a twin? What is life like? The lovely poem, 'My twin and I" traces the intimate bonds and interesting events in the childhood years of a set of identical twins. How does their life change as they enter adulthood? What do they wish for as they move into their senior years? Read on/ Listen in?

Poem

We felt something so close
Too close, yet so comforting…
Part of one's own, yet apart
What was it?
Soft and fleshy
That sometimes
Nudged and kicked?
Did we learn to love
This other part?
To live and let live
Even whilst in the womb?

A green band on my wrist
While on the other's, 'twas blue
Frothy feeds in warm bottles.
Timed to whosoever finished first!
"Was it Blue or was it Green?"
Who did I just now feed?
Whose turn is it now?"
A kind, vigilant face, asked....
It was 'Mother'!
She checked the band
On the wrist
Before placing
The succulent nipple
On the pouting lip...

We learnt to bawl louder,
Kicking tiny legs
To holler high...
Each screaming,
"Damned the band,
I am hungry still!"
We grew months
And years older
Yet, confusion continued
To confound most...
Written bold and large
On faces new and old !

"Who was this?
Was it him or me?"
They called him me
When he was not
And called me, him
When I was not!
Like two peas in a pod
Like mirror images perfect,
We became a test
Of observation,
Of realization…
To know how different
Was the tip of his nose
Or for that matter,
The curve of my smile!

We quickly learnt how to trick
Every outsider, just outright!
When one was absent
She marked the other, so!
He did not do his homework
And she made me stand
Up, on the back bench so bald.
He topped the test
But I, proudly, paraded
The medal pinned
On my vest!

'He and his mirror'
As they called
Me and my brother!
Blurred images…
Mistaken identities
At times frustrating,
Many a time, hilarious!
And we learnt to love,
To live and to let live!

We wore identical colours
Prints and cuts, the very same…
Everything was always in twos
Forever in doubles
One for the each of us.
Our names too
Were called at once, together,
In one single breath…
Like a compound word
Co-joined, continuous…
One incomplete, lame,
Without, the other.

Time distanced us
As did our inclinations…
His preference
Over mine…
A little similar,

Yet distinct, different…
And as one grew
A millimeter taller
More, than the other;
The other voice soon,
Changed and turned
Just a tad, gruffier too!
While one moustache
Lo! Wasn't as rebellious though!
Yet… we seemed
And remained,
The very same…
Still felt together;
Alike, much like the other;
And loved being together.

But destiny did do us apart
Left us far and distanced
From our beginnings
In the warm womb;
Land masses large
Seas and oceans betwixt!
Life has, mountain like, changed…
Still, the 'wombly' connection
Taut and intact, remains;
It sudden, tugs the heart,
Twinging, painful, apart.

Even as we journey along
High and low,
Through thick and thin;
Even as we step
Into our silver years,
A deep reckoning
Boldly rises, deep within…
We awaken, seeking,
Our alter egos, beckoning…
On many a long night,
At hours, so very wee…
We feel the pulse and beat
Of the other half
Floating so close
Just as it was
Decades ago,
Dark and hazy though…
Just as it was,
Huddled tight, together
In the cosy comfort
Of our creator,
Our Mother's core
And we look

Look for each other
For each other,
As never ever
Before!

Towards Her

Password: Listn22me?

19

Towards Her

Preface

Set in the background of a temple, the poem describes the poet's internal conflict. Two attractions draw him in opposing directions and he struggles with them. What are they? What is the final resolution? Read on/ listen in to find out……

Story in Verse

I sat....
Hands folded; statue like
In the orange–red light
Of the greasy oil lamp……
Her anointed face,
-Turmeric and sandal-
Awe inspiring, shone bright…

Her spectacular nose-stud
Dazzled diamond rays
In dozens of stars;
Even as
Rose scented vapours

Haloed a perfumed haze
In her sacred chamber
The sanctum……

When a new
Bright orange light
Breezed past me,
I sudden turned
And saw another 'her'
On my right
Leaning on the railing

Beside the long aisle……
She glowed,
Brilliant; like her
In the sanctum;
The very same
Turmeric and red hues
The perfume of roses
Hanging luscious,
On curly locks!

I took a deep breath
-Even as her scent whiffed
Into my being-
And swung my gaze back
At her
In the sanctum.

I closed my eyes.
To focus on her,
The Almighty, The Divine!

Images floated and danced…
My mental eye
Now, their welcome stage!
She, from inside the sanctum
Beckoned with a smile
But at that very moment
I was blinded
By the other her!
Her million watt smile!
I wanted to
Touch and hold
Her cupped hands
Perfumed with petals, pink
As she leaned eagerly,
Continued to lean,
On the railing.

My gaze,
Remained transfixed
On her, standing,
On the outside,
To my right…
I was hypnotized…

For how long?
I knew not!

And then
I sudden,
Regained my senses…
I turned…
Turned with a huge sigh
Or was it relief?
I turned back to see
The Goddess inside
And to feel her grace.

A few seconds passed
Oh Fie!
I could not hold on…
My mind flip-flopped…
Jelly like;
It ran amuck……
Like mercury
It darted back and forth
Between the inside
And the outside
She or Her?
Who did I
Seek and yearn for?

I chided my fickle,
Temptation stricken head
And tried
To fix myself
On a straight gaze......
I was lost to the world
For some counts of time
Riveted On Her,
Glowing in the sanctum.

Soon it seems,
My focus
Once more, slipped...
My neck,
In auto mode,
Veered to the right
To the railing...
And drew a blank.

My eyes blinked
And then gaped
In disbelief.
I could not
See her!
She was gone
Yes! Really!

Out of sight!
Where? How?
When did she go?
Helpless and lost
I looked straight
At Her, for help.
"Please let me find her!"
"Please, Please!"
My hands folded
In hope and in a plea,
I closed my eyes tight
As my lips chanted
A prayer.

The bells tolled
To the rhythm
Of the chant
Loud and clear
And to rising crescendos
Of voices ringing a shriek…
"Bagawathi Amme
Amme… Amme"
I stood mesmerized
For I don't know
How long
But when I opened
My eyes

Lo behold!
The image grew vivid…
I saw that
Alluring face!
That million watts smile!
Those petal filled hands!

But where was she?

Looking at the inside
Had I lost her?
Or, had she come back?
My breath found
An unknown excitement
The gentle breeze tingled
And made my hair
Stand on end;
My quickening pulse
Paced without restraint;
I turned my head
And looked for her
At that same spot
On my right
But she was not there.
And as I turned
And looked
For her inside,

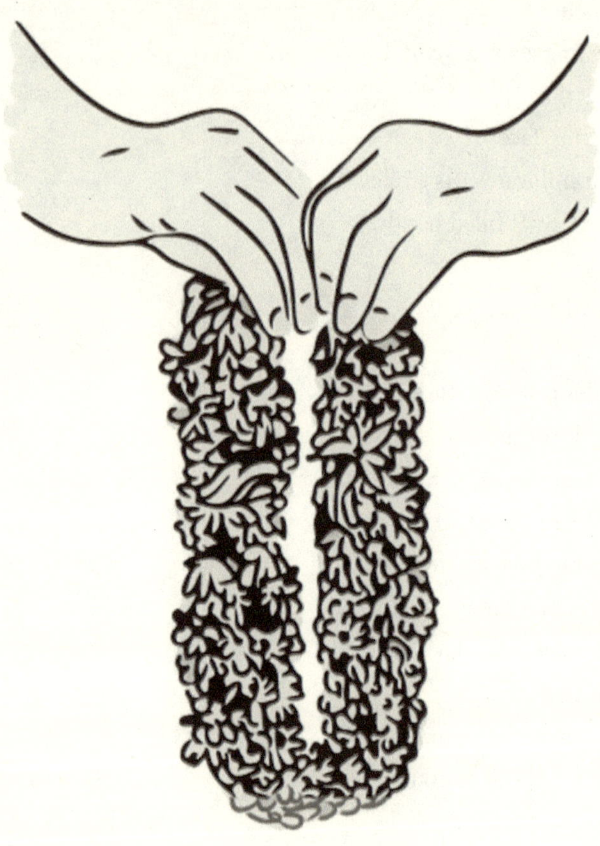

I felt her presence
Strong and clear
Like real
Everywhere…
In every breath
In every beat…
Both inside the sanctum

And outside
Leaning on the railing…
All over… omnipresent-
Smiling and beckoning
I gripped the garland
Tight, in my hands
And, in a trance
Floated
Towards Her.

Now at 43

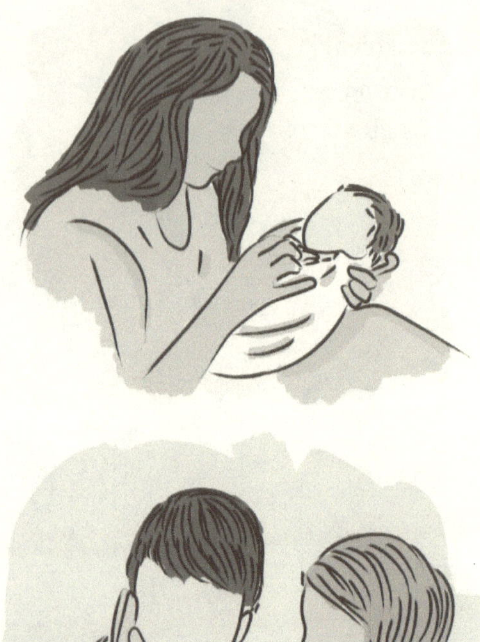

Password: Listn22me?

20

Now at 43

Preface

In the poem set to rhyme, 'Now at 43', the poet reminisces the birth of her son and describes her emotions when she held him for the very first time. What does she feel on his 43rd birthday and what are her wishes for him? Read on/ Listen in…

Poem

A cuddly curved ball,
You spilled out of me, in full bawl;
'He's a boy', she let out a cry,
Ruffling my soaked sheets, to look up, I did try.
Red and wet, shrieking in full,
Angry to be disturbed, like a bull;
Booming cries that rent the air
Your arrival into my life, you did declare!
Now three and forty years later,
The image does not falter;
Oh! How can I describe the feel,

As I beheld and bonded a seal?
Is my child a bright bonny boy?
Healthy to enjoy every earthly joy?
My heart tossed in nervous scare
Even as my eyes on you, locked in a stare.
I then sudden, felt you close to my chest
And at that moment, every fear was laid to rest.

It did not matter if you were very short
Or many of my dreams, you would thwart;
It did not matter if you were so very far
That I'd have to look for you in every long star;
It wouldn't matter what you ever were
If being so ordinary, you never caused any stir!
For, when I held you close to myself,
All time and purpose seemed to find itself!
My life had found a deep core, a centre
A new hope, a joy to tender and to render.
I raised you not to keep or my line to toe
But to set you free and see how you grow;
Watch you from afar, and help you make a life
Seek and find every joy with your soulful wife.
You are now a full man, at forty-three
But nothing has changed even a wee degree.
My child is what I saw on that day

Forty-three years ago, today!
And that is how I will forever, you, see…
Be you forty, sixty or eighty-three!
Bless you today, on your special day
And wish you many many happy returns of this day!

Those Pink Envelopes

Password: Listn22me?

21

Those Pink Envelopes

Preface

Those Pink Envelopes is a delightful story poem about a young student's struggle with first love. How does he design ingenious ways and means to express his feelings? What happens thereafter? Read on/ listen in.

Story in Verse

Pink Christmas lights flashed,
Bright and iridescent
On the large glass windows
Of my office
In downtown, Seattle…
Sipping black coffee
I stood at the
Bay windows
And peered
Into the pink haze
That had enveloped
Earth and heavens,
Trees and skies
All around……

The pink aura
Set them off…
Images of pink envelopes
Small and big
Square and rectangle…
Spilled out of my head
Each one of them
Etched in memory
Clear… distinct… specific…
Up to the date and time
When I had slipped
Each under the door
Her name
Beautifully calligraphed
On the pink face
Of the crisp envelope.

My mind jumped
Recklessly,
Shuffling chronology
And logic…
I was standing
Outside the door…
She was inside
With my mom,
Locked in conversation
For what appeared, ages.

And then,
Mom came out,
Marching cheerfully,
With a mysterious smile
Stuck on her
'Lip-sticked' lips,
Bright pink!
A stack of pink envelopes
Balanced at her elbow
Precariously
As she jingled
Her bangled forearm
And waltzed
To the car-park…
I could do nothing else
But follow her
Quiet and quick.
Like a mouse…

'Oh my God!
She had my
Precious pink treasures!
How to reclaim them?
And why is she smiling?
All lit up in evil glee?
I burst forth
With a volley of questions…

But all I got
Was a terse response…
"I will tell you
Now I have to rush"
She had got into the car
And whisked off
With my pink envelopes!
My entire being
Had seared
In an unknown ache
For hours.

My train of thought
Time travelled
Further back…
To the day
When I had
Gotten on to that
Emotional roller coaster…
It was the first day
Of my final year
At school
When I saw her
For the first time…
And until that day
I had never seen
Anyone quite like her!

Her plum silken kurta
Gave her ivory skin
A golden sheen…
Her million watts smile
Blinded all senses…
Petite and chic
Wearing stiletto heels
Breaking many a stereo type,
She looked more a model
Than a teacher!
I simply could not
Get past
My new English teacher…
She consumed
My thoughts
And time
And possessed
My entire being
I felt a different person
Altogether, from the day
I set my eyes on her.

The infatuation!
The obsession!
Changed me
Drastically…
I had to

Share my feelings
With her
And that was how
The story of
The pink envelopes
Began……

I tried hard
To win her attention
In class
But became quite
A laughing stock
In the bargain.
I strongly felt
She knew…
Knew
How awestruck
I was,
Of her…
But she
Deftly avoided
Meeting me
In the eye…
So I stopped
Trying to draw
Her attention…
To talk out of turn
To irritate her

To exasperate,
Just to hear her
Call out my name.
Instead, I spent hours
Yes… literally hours
Sketching and painting
Birds, bees, flowers
All in twos, in pairs…
Couples by the seaside
On mountain tops
In railway coupes
In parks
On giant wheels……
I was going
Just crazy!
I put each
Of my creations
Into a bright pink
Envelope;
I carefully
Cut and made
Lovely envelopes
In different sizes
And shapes
As I could not
Lay hands on them,
Readymade!

I would then
Write her name
Above each drawing.
In different calligraphic styles
With special pens
Then I would carefully seal
The envelope
And decorate her name
With elegant stroke
And flourish!
What ingenuity
It was to find
Ways and means
To hide and slide
My creations
Under the door…

That mighty
Oak and brass
Façade
That stood
Majestic
On the corridor…
Guarding
The privacy
Of her room!
I would then let
My imagination
Run riot…
Images of her
Admiring my drawing
And smiling
Appeared even
In my dreams…
Accepting the envelope
Became an acceptance of me
Or so, I deluded myself
But in those days
It all seemed so real
So urgent
So important!

I watched her closely,
To observe any change
In her attitude to me

Was she friendlier?
Or was she cross?
Was there a change
In her voice?
A flutter?
An extra warmth?
Did she look at me?
In class, differently?

I frequently
Changed positions
To check this out.
But all was in vain
She was just the same
Matter of fact
Void of highs and lows…
I was just another student
A cog in a wheel
Although by now
I had painstakingly
Given her 20 envelopes
At least…
I was a bundle of emotions
Often so contradictory…
Excitement, craving attention
On one side
Anxiety and fear
On the other……

Distracted, unable to focus
Grades plummeting
Feeling hopeless
And helpless
Most of the time…
Above all
My mind
Was constantly
In doubt…
Did she know
It was me?
Did she guess?
Did she want to find out?
Will she report me?
Will I be suspended?
Sometimes nightmares
Made we wake up
All sweaty and exhausted.

But it was all silent and quiet!
There was just no reaction
She never looked me
In the eye
And that seemed
Such a betrayal…
Wasn't some reaction
Good or bad
Better than none?

I tried to ask my mom
About the pink envelopes
"What did madam say?"
"Nothing much"
"Anything about me?"
"Not really......
Finish your exams
And then we can talk...
Don't waste time now"

And then, I could bear it no more
I decided to talk to her
"Ma'am can I speak to you?"
"Yes what?"
"Ma'am about those pink envelopes..."
"Oh Yes...
What about them?"
There was no look
Of surprise in her eyes or voice
So, she had known all along!
"Well... Ma'am I really......"
"Yes I too really..." she cut me short...
"I think
You are very good
In art and in calligraphy...
I have given your mom
A list of colleges you can go to

To study Art and Design
I really like your drawings.
Now run along
I have to go……"

Having sailed
Tempestuous seas
Oh hope and passion
For months on…
I was abruptly
Thrown out of
Fantasy world!
My love boat
Tumbled and capsized…
I landed back
On dark, dusty earth…
Despondent and angry,
I mopped around
As though I had
Lost the world
But no one gave me
A second look……
The final nail
In the coffin
Of unrequited love
Was hammered
When she left school

Soon after,
Reportedly, to get married!

Lost in reminiscence,
I walked back
From the window
To my desk
And looked at
My name plate
That dazzled on it……
'Creative Director'
I read it aloud
Feeling happy and proud…
So proud of her
Who had spotted my talent…
So grateful to her
For being my teacher
A teacher to the core…
For not complaining
About my
Moon struck madness…

For saving me from
Embarrassment and reprimand
For shaping my future
With such vision,
Such wisdom

And goodwill!
I saluted her
For the nth time
And walked
Into the pink mist.

To Meet with Him

Password: Listn22me?

22

To Meet with Him

Preface

In the beautiful, soul searching poem, 'To Meet with Him', the poet describes her first meeting with Him, whom she had always felt a deep connection. Why is she is waiting in the House of God to meet with Him? What is her feeling? What is her seek? Read on to find out.

Poem

I had heard of him
For years,
Ever since a child…
His resplendence
His grace
His majesty
The way a hundred elephants
Came together
To herald his presence.
To greet him
With fireworks and fan fare
Decorated in caparisons and parasols
Dazzling gold and light…
For years, I had waited…

Waited to 'experience' Him
To soak in Him......
On that day,
With flutters in my heart
And a tickle in my veins,
I sat with myself,
Ensconced,
On the high grey stone
Of the long corridor
With slim, carved pillars
And earthen, tiled roofs...
The stony surface,
Was comforting...
Polished and smooth
By hundreds of feet
And butts
The had
Rubbed on them,
For centuries.

In front of me,
Layers of circular lamps
Piled on each other,
Began to glow...
Their black lips,
Moist and slippery;
Soot filled and oily...,
They glimmered
Yellow and red...

In defiant match
To the orange glow
Of the setting sun.
The last *myna
Nesting on the Peepal
Homed in
In flurry and hurry,
Just as the first note
Of the *nadaswaram
Set off
From
Crafted breath…
Even as the soft beat
Of the Tavil
Sprung; definite
Yet, in step…

Soon, the blare
Of windy music
And the pulse
Of tapping fingers
Striking hard on
Seasoned skin
Rent the air
That was already
Throbbing
In full throttle
With the chant…
'Sadashiva

Shiva
Om
Sadasiva,
Shiva
Om'!

The refrain,
In mixed voices,
Both soprano
And baritone
Blended with
Nadaswaram,
Thavil
And human tongues…
A screeching child
A doting mother
The impatient husband
The fervent old lady
All united in their mission
To see past bobbing heads…
To catch a glimpse
Of the manifest form
Of primordial energy
Of Him,
The Creator!

I continued to sit
In the festive, wedding like
Ambience…

And soaked in its
Auspiciousness
For a prolonged count
Of 'earthly time';
Forgetting them all…
My trials
My triumphs;
My needs
My hopes
My fears
My bonds;
I clutched the pillar
To drop a descent…
Descend down
And go under,
To leave behind,
My Entity,
My Self,
To drop and
To rise in flight,
A flight of consciousness…
To mingle with
The throng of Life
To get past it all!
To meet with
That Supreme Spirit
In stone…

In the dark
Womb like, sanctum…
To meet,
And to merge…
To connect,
And to coincide
To coincide
And to remain.
To remain
In complete communion....
In union
With HIM
The only HIM,
THE VADAKKUNATHAN!*

*VADAKKUNATHAN is the presiding diety in the famous Shiva temple in Trichur – Kerala India
*Myna is a bird that is native to India and southern Asia
*Nadaswaram is a double reed wind instrument from South India.

www.ingramcontent.com/pod-product-compliance
Lightning Source LLC
LaVergne TN
LVHW091204150826
845672LV00005B/1236

* 9 7 9 8 8 9 2 7 7 9 5 7 9 *